Introducing
THE KINGDOM OF
FIFE

Jack Forrest

**with photographs by
Dennis Hardley**

and St Andrews

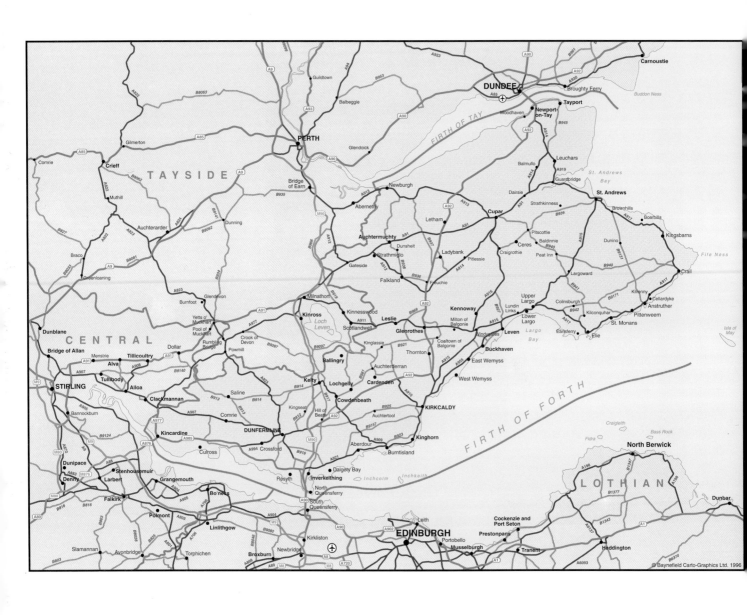

INTRODUCING
The Kingdom of Fife

All of Scotland is rich in history and heritage but, in the Kingdom of Fife there is a certain something which brings visitors back time and time again.

Perhaps some of the most attractive qualities of Fife are the surprises which are around every corner. This Kingdom is certainly one of the least discovered areas of Scotland and it is easy to understand why those in the know are often reluctant to advertise their secret. Let me give you some examples:

Everyone has heard of St Andrews as a golfing Mecca but, did you know that, in Fife, there are more than 35 golf courses ranging from ones whose green fees are under £10 to those of championship standard, several of which are used regularly for the qualifying rounds of The Open? If fishing is more down your stream you may be surprised to know that there are more than 20 fishing locations in Fife. You can catch brown trout, rainbow trout, sea trout and salmon in Fife's lochs and rivers, in the comfortable knowledge that you won't have to share your spot with hoards of fellow fishermen.

Another well kept secret is the Isle of May, five miles off the mainland. During the summer season there is a regular ferry service to the island, home to thousands of puffins who have long known about the island's beauty – as they say, 40,000 puffins can't be wrong! They seem to welcome visitors as do the seals who will come to meet your boat and escort it to the landing jetty. Keeping to the seaside theme, there is, in Fife, a village whose beaches face in every direction making it possible to be sheltered from sea breezes at all times, if sun bathing is more to your taste; and, talking about sun bathing did you know that Fife has more days of sun than Scarborough and less of rain than the Isle of Wight, a comforting thought when there are no less than five beaches which hold the coveted 1996 Seaside Award?

Not content with boasting one ancient capital, Fife has two. Dunfermline, the seat of Scotland's early Celtic kings was capital long before Edinburgh. Here twenty two kings, queens, princes and princesses are buried in the grounds of Dunfermline Abbey, the Westminster of the North. Further north lies St Andrews which was, before the reformation the ecclesiastical capital of Scotland. It took builders more than 150 years to complete the construction of the largest cathedral ever to be built in Scotland and now, more than 8 centuries later visitors still marvel at the awesome enormity of the ruins.

These are a few of Fife's secrets – there are many more just waiting to be discovered. What is not a secret, however, is the welcome you will receive when you arrive in the Kingdom of Fife. Whether you will tell anyone about it when you return home is up to you.

KINGDOM OF
FIFE
TOURIST BOARD

DAVID McINTYRE
CHIEF EXECUTIVE
Kingdom of Fife Tourist Board

For five hundred years this beautiful area was the centre of royal and political life in Scotland. Its geographical position on the north of the Firth of Forth offered not only access for shipping and trade, but defence from the north and south and fertile lands for pasture and crops. This ancient Kingdom therefore offers the visitor much to revisit in the pages of history and a feast of visitor attractions, theatres and nature trails which will appeal to all members of the family.

Fife is easily reached however you travel. Edinburgh airport is less than an hours drive away and there are excellent coach and bus connections from the central belt and further north. Although Fife is quickly

Opposite: *Pittencrieff Park, Dunfermline gifted to the people of the town from the Pittencrieff Estate by Andrew Carnegie in 1903.*

Right: *Dunfermline Abbey, a legacy from mediaeval times and 19th century 'Gothic' architecture.*

Above: *The Mercat Cross in the 17th century village Culross.*

Right: *Some of the restored buildings in Culross, including the Tolbooth.*

accessible from the main A90 and M90 roads, visitors soon find themselves driving along country roads and through unspoiled towns and villages which reflect the remarkable history of this area.

The town of Dunfermline was Scotland's capital for

Opposite: *The world famous Forth Rail Bridge, completed in 1890 after seven years of labour, spans the Firth of Forth between North and South Queensferry.*

half a millennia and that past unfolds in this still bustling town as you explore the 12th century Abbey; still in use today, the ruins of the Royal Palace or the 11th century Canmore's Tower, named after Malcolm Canmore, who ruled Scotland during that time. The most famous of all Scottish Kings, Robert the Bruce, is buried in Dunfermline.

The renowned benefactor Andrew Carnegie was born here in 1835. Said to be "the man of steel with a heart of gold", Carnegie's story was an epic of rags to riches as he forged his $400 million fortune in the furnaces of Pittsburgh, USA. Today there are four separate Carnegie Trusts, which spend an estimated $100 million a year supporting innovative schemes and many

individual beneficiaries. The Andrew Carnegie Birthplace Museum tells his remarkable story. Dunfermline offers the visitor a successful blend of

Above: *The peaceful harbour at Dysart, near Kirkcaldy.*

Opposite: *Fine buildings near Dysart harbour at the Pan Ha', where salt pans once stood.*

Scotland's great heritage mixed with modern amenities and accommodation. Just north of Dunfermline on the A823 is Knockhill Racing Circuit which guarantees an exciting and interesting day out.

Linking the towns in Fife are many peaceful scenic roads including an unspoiled coastline affording views over the Firth of Forth to Edinburgh and beyond. Each town or village encountered along the route has its own charm and story to tell.

Aberdour, with its 14th century castle to explore, also gives the opportunity of

Above and opposite: *The harbour at Elie dates back to 1582. Today it is popular with watersports enthusiasts and local fishermen. The village is well worth a visit especially for golfers.*

a boat ride to Inchcolm Island and its ancient priory. The domestic architecture of Culross, much of it in the care of the National Trust for Scotland, is a delightful place in which to wander, and at North Queensferry there is an excellent sailing centre and a unique aquarium featuring an underwater tunnel and lots of fun for children and adults.

Queensferry was named after Queen Margaret, the wife of King Malcolm. She personally funded a ferry across the Firth of Forth which saved pilgrims from the south of Scotland a tortuous journey round the Firth to worship at the many holy places in Fife. The Queen was later canonised and became known as Saint Margaret.

Kirkcaldy is the main shopping centre of the "Kingdom" and is home to the famous links market

reputed to be the largest street fair in Europe. In its environs there are many parks and gardens which are popular with picnickers, and the Beveridge Park has its own boating lake and extensive tree lined walks. Kirkcaldy is also the location for many forms of entertainment - The Adam Smith theatre, named after one of Fife's famous sons Adam Smith, hosts musicals, plays and films. The Museum and Art Gallery has a fine collection of

paintings by S. J. Peploe and William MacTaggart.

Burntisland has been a popular destination for day trippers and holiday-makers alike for many years. Its well-kept links area is the venue for the summer funfair and many other spectacular arena events throughout the season. A short distance away, Kinghorn was created as a royal burgh in the 12th

Opposite: The Parish Church at St Monans was built by David II between 1362-70. The clifftop graveyard contains the remains of mariners from times past.

Above: *Kellie Castle near Pittenweem is an excellent example of Jacobean architecture, carefully restored by Sir James Lorimer in 1878.*

century and is a picturesque and ideal location for sailing and watersports in general. This lovely town, which has been a magnet for visitors for many years, also boasts tennis courts, bowling and an excellent 18 hole golf course. Kinghorn Loch and Pettycur sands are also firm family favourites.

The south coast of Fife is particularly famed for its

picturesque fishing villages and towns which were once the centre of Scotland's shipping trade. These towns continue to recount the story of Scotland's past in their many castles, towers and fine houses which were home to successive Kings and Queens, as well as offering an array of activities.

Driving along this delightful coast, with its panoramic views across to Edinburgh and beyond, the visitor is forced to take a step back in time in the ancient villages of

Above: *A very typical Fife scene at Pittenweem harbour.*

Right: *A delightful row of cottages by the beach at Pittenweem.*

Opposite: *A picturesque scene looking down on Pittenweem from the cliffs.*

Dysart and East and West Wemyss. Now a haven for small boats, Dysart once saw elegant tall ships in her harbour bringing wine, pantiles and general cargoes from the Netherlands, and sailing away again with coal and salt for far-off countries.

A panoramic view of the beach and the world famous Fife town of St Andrews.

The village is steeped in character with its charming streets fronted by old houses with traditional crow-stepped gables including "Pan Ha'", 17th century fisher houses which have been masterfully restored by the National Trust for Scotland. Dysart was also the birthplace of John McDouall Stuart, the man who first explored Australia and a museum in the village provides a fitting tribute to his exploits. East and West Wemyss each have their own distinctive features, including McDuff Castle in East Wemyss reputed to be the home of the MacDuff in Shakespeare's MacBeth.

The seaside town of Leven is also a very popular tourist destination. With its spectacular new swimming pool, leisure complex and traditional sandy beaches, it is an ideal location for families and this is reflected in its programme of entertainment which includes a veteran car rally and a stream of professional entertainers. The promenade with its putting greens, paddling pool and

Above and opposite: *Anstruther, home of the Scottish Fisheries Museum, was once also home to a large sailing fleet whose ships plied the Baltic and Mediterranean for cargo. Later it also boasted a huge herring fishing fleet.*

amusement arcades is the ideal venue for many of these activities.

Fife's fishing and shipping ancestry is perhaps best illustrated in the picture-postcard villages of Elie, St Monans, Pittenweem, Anstruther and Crail. Situated on that part of the south coast called the East Neuk ("neuk" is the old Scots word for corner), these remarkable villages were the centre of

Above and opposite: *Crail is arguably one of the most photographed villages in Scotland. The village is one of the oldest royal burghs dating back to 1178 and its picturesque harbour is reputed to have been built by Dutch women engineers.*

Scotland's trade with Scandinavian countries in mediaeval times when goods such as wool, coal and leather were exchanged for timber and manufactured goods. In the 19th and early 20th century, fishing became

the main occupation with the establishment of the colourful herring industry. Now, although fishing is still in existence, the pace is unhurried and peaceful with each village seemingly immune from the passage of time. With their small white-washed houses, which still retain much of their Flemish influence, and winding streets leading down to secluded harbours, it is little

Above: *A view of St Andrews from the south with St Rule's Tower and the beach.*

Opposite: *A splendid view of St Andrews from St Rule's Tower which overlooks the grounds of the cathedral, the site of one thousand years of Christian pilgrimage.*

Top left & right: *St Andrews Cathedral was once the second largest church in Britain. University students relax in the Cathedral grounds.*

Above: *The Swilcan Bridge over the burn of the same name at St Andrews Royal and Ancient Golf Club.*

wonder that these villages are among the most photographed in Scotland.

On the east coast of Fife is the distinguished town of St Andrews. It is famed of course for its "Old Course" golf links, but in addition to the vast golfing complex and its place as the "Home of Golf", St Andrew's has a wealth of history and entertainment to offer all visitors. This ancient Royal Burgh is without doubt one of the great historic cities of Europe, attracting visitors since the religious pilgrims of the Celtic faith. Legend has it that relics of the apostle, St Andrew, were brought to Scotland by St Regulus who was shipwrecked off the Fife coast and founded a church where the town now stands.

Right: *A blanket of colour in one of the village gardens at Leuchars.*

Opposite: *The boating lake at Craigtoun Country Park on the outskirts of St Andrews.*

Opposite: *Tayport harbour on Fife's north coast used to be the rail ferry point for the journey across the Tay to Broughty Ferry before the days of the rail bridge.*

Above: *A view across the Tay Estuary towards the City of Dundee from Wormit. The Tay Rail Bridge carries the main line from London Kings Cross to Dundee and Aberdeen. Opened on 11 July 1887, it is 3135m long and carries two tracks.*

The first rail bridge collapsed on the night of 28 December 1879 during a winter storm. The crew and 75 passengers of a train crossing the bridge lost their lives on that ill-fated night.

St Andrew was then to become the Patron Saint of Scotland.

St Andrews is home to Scotland's oldest university and other important historic landmarks such as its cathedral, castle and harbour are found among the mediaeval, Victorian and Edwardian streets. Shops, restaurants, theatres and art galleries abound, and an array of fairs, festivals and pageants means that there is always a varied programme of events on offer.

Travelling north from St Andrews there are more towns and villages to explore in this area, including Leuchars with its long association with the RAF. It is also however home of the 12th century Church of

Opposite: In the care of the National Trust for Scotland, Hill of Tarvit near Cupar was originally designed in 1696 as Wemyss Hall. It has a fine collection of furniture, paintings and tapestries.

Right: Many of Falkland's original buildings have been restored in this Conservation Area of Scotland including the decorative Victorian letter-box.

St Athernase, one of finest examples of Norman architecture in Britain. In the 19th century this north coast of Fife was a very fashionable place for the jute barons of Fife to reside.

Again history abounds; from Tentsmuir where there were known to be stone age and bronze age people living, to the tragedy of the Tay Rail Bridge disaster of 1879 when the northbound train

plummeted into the River Tay killing 75 passengers as the bridge collapsed.

Moving inland visitors immediately become aware of the importance which agriculture has played in the traditions of Fife. The Lomond Hills, in the area known as the "Howe of Fife", always popular with walkers and ramblers, rise majestically from richly fertile fields and woodlands. The hills of Cleish and Benarty are also popular with visitors and there are inland angling facilities at nearby Loch Leven. There is evidence too of some of Fife's more recent industrial history of limekilns and coal mining. The new town of Glenrothes in the heartland of Fife, has much in the way of all-weather

Kingdom of Fife Tourist Board.

Right: *Iris sculptures at The Kingdom Centre, Glenrothes.*

Opposite: *Falkland Palace is a royal hunting lodge dating back to King James IV c.1500. The buildings feature a variety of architectural styles and include a 16th century royal tennis court, which is one of only two in the UK to survive from that time.*

activities. Practically every sports interest is catered for, with indoor and outdoor bowling, horse riding, golf and a swimming pool and

sports centre. The new Rothes Halls always has a full calendar of arts events on offer. The village of Falkland, with its beautiful Palace, is nearby. The town gained fame in the 14th century through its association with the Stewart monarchy but later, even without that royal presence, Falkland prospered in the spinning and weaving of flax.

Fife has always been important religiously and royally, but many of its sons and daughters have also gained fame throughout the world. Carnegie, John McDouall Stuart and Robert Adam, the renowned architect, have already been

mentioned in these pages, but worthy of note too are Adam Smith, the man who founded the science of political economy, Thomas Carlyle, who no doubt influenced a few of Kirkcaldy's pupils and Mary Sommerville, the internationally acclaimed scientific writer.

The Kingdom of Fife is a wonderful place to visit. Its dynamic place in Scottish history has left an array of grand castles, palaces and houses, and fine cathedrals,

abbeys and churches. The sons and daughters of Fife have also played an important part in that history with a host of pioneers and champions whose lives are celebrated in towns and villages around the area. However, combined with those important historic links, Fife offers family fun in its miles of sandy beaches and associated activities, a huge selection of sporting pursuits and a choice of delightful villages to explore at your leisure.

KINGDOM OF
FIFE
TOURIST BOARD

Head Office: 7 Hanover Court Glenrothes Fife KY7 5SB
Tel: 01592 750066 Fax: 01592 611180
St. Andrews, Crail, Anstruther, Leven, Kirkcaldy, Burntisland, Forth Bridges, Dunfermline, Cupar